Real Science-

Level II

Laboratory Workbook

Dr. R. W. Keller

RealScience
4
Kids

Cover design: David Keller
Opening page: David Keller, Rebecca Keller
Illustrations: Rebecca Keller

Real Science-4-Kids: Chemistry Level II-Laboratory Workbook

ISBN 9780976509790

Published by Gravitas Publications, Inc.
P.O. Box 4790
Albuquerque, NM 87196-4790

Printed in the United States

GRAVITAS
PUBLICATIONS INC

ON YOUR OWN - About Level II Experiments
(a note from the author)

All of the experiments for Level II Chemistry are essentially "on your own." One of the most essential features of science is the ability to problem solve and create new ideas. You can't do this unless you try. There are often not many chances in life to try new ideas, so I decided to let Level II experiments be created by you, the student.

At first this is going to be frustrating. Staring at a blank "Experiment" with only a hint or two to go on is going to seem unfair. You may be nervous about doing it "right" or you may be confused about how to get started. To ease you into the idea, I have written most of the first three experiments for you, but by Experiment 4, you are entirely on your own. The teacher's manual contains a "Sample Experiment" for all ten chapters if you get really stuck, but resist the temptation to simply follow the teacher's recipe - what do they know?

It may seem odd for a scientist to say this, but there is no one right way to do an experiment. There are better ways to test a hypothesis just as there are better ways to stick a note to your mom on the corner of her computer screen (Which is best? - duct tape, scotch tape, Elmer's glue, super glue, bubble gum or Post-Its? Did you know that the glue on Post-its was glue that "didn't work"). So yes, there are better ways to do everything, but that is why you have to "experiment" to find out what works best.

Most importantly, have fun. You get to do your own experiments and in the process I hope you will *discover* real science.

Rebecca W. Keller, Ph.D.

Laboratory Safety

Most of these experiments use household items. However, some items, such as iodine, are extremely poisonous. Extra care should be taken while working with all chemicals in this series of experiments. The following are some general laboratory precautions that should be applied to the home laboratory:

Never put things in your mouth without explicit instructions to do so. This means that food items should not be eaten unless tasting or eating is part of the experiment.

Use safety glasses while using glass objects or strong chemicals such as bleach.

Wash hands before and after handling chemicals.

Use adult supervision while working with iodine and while conducting any step requiring a stove.

Contents

Experiment 1:   Low Sodium   1

Experiment 2:   Building Molecules   5

Experiment 3:   Mass Matters   9

Experiment 4:   Acids and Bases   17

Experiment 5:   Neutralization Reactions   23

Experiment 6:   To Mix or not to Mix   29

Experiment 7:   Pigments in Plant   35

Experiment 8:   Testing Food for Carbohydrates and Lipids   41

Experiment 9:   Crosslinking Polymers   47

Experiment 10:   Which has more DNA? An onion or an egg?   53

Nucleic Acid Extraction Protocol   59

EXPERIMENT 1:   LOW SODIUM

You go to the familiy doctor and he decides to put you on a special diet. He tells you that you have been eating too much sodium. He is an old chemist and he tells you not to eat more than 0.01 moles of sodium per day. This sounds pretty easy, until you go home and find out that all of the food items list the amount of sodium in mg (milligrams). How do you follow the doctor's orders? Which foods can you eat?

HINTS:

First determine the atomic weight of sodium. It is on the periodic chart and the quantity is given as grams per mole (grams/mole). Record this quantity here _____

Remember that the atomic weight tells you how many grams of an element are in one mole. But you need to find out how many milligrams are in 0.01 moles. To find out how many milligrams of sodium are in 0.01 moles, first convert grams of sodium in one mole to milligrams of sodium (1000 milligram = 1 grams) in one mole and then mulitply by 0.01 moles. This will give you milligrams of sodium in 0.01 moles.

Do your calculation here:

milligrams (mg) of sodium in 0.01 moles = _____

Now set up your experiment.

Experiment 1: _____   Date: _____

Objective: _____

Hypothesis: _____

I. List the Materials you need:

MATERIALS

II. Write out the steps of your experiment in as much detail as possible.

EXPERIMENT

1. _____
   _____
   _____

2. _____
   _____
   _____

3. _____
   _____
   _____

4. _____
   _____

5. _____
   _____
   _____

III. Record your results.

RESULTS

Food Item	Serving size	Sodium (in milligrams)

_____
_____
_____
_____
_____
_____
_____
_____
_____
_____

IV. Discuss your results and write your conclusions.

CONCLUSIONS

_____

_____

_____

_____

_____

_____

_____

_____

_____

_____

_____

_____

_____

_____

_____

_____

_____

_____

_____

_____

EXPERIMENT 2:   BUILDING MOLECULES

You need to explain to your mom, dad, younger, or older siblings how molecular bonds are formed. To do this you need to build models so they can understand how atoms combine to form molecular bonds.

Experiment 2: _____   Date: _____

Objective: _____

Hint: Review Appendix A and carefully study all of the different ways atoms combine to form molecules.

Before you begin collecting items for your models, think about the two different kinds of bonds you need to illustrate (ionic and covalent). What would you need to demonstrate these two types of bonds?

Next, think about the kinds of molecular bonding orbitals for covalent bonds (sigma and pi). How could you build models to demonstrate these?

Finally think about the different kinds of hybrid orbitals (sp, sp^2 sp^3) that form some covalent bonds. What would you need to make models for these?

I. List the Materials you need:

MATERIALS

_____
_____
_____
_____
_____
_____
_____
_____
_____
_____
_____

II. Write out the steps of your experiment in as much detail as possible.
Hint: List the names of molecules you will use to demonstrate (e.g. NaCl, H_2 etc.)

EXPERIMENT

1. _____
_____

2. _____
_____

3. _____
_____

4. _____
_____

5. _____
_____

6. _____
_____
_____
_____
_____
_____
_____
_____
_____
_____
_____
_____

III. Record your results.

RESULTS

_____

_____

_____

_____

_____

_____

_____

_____

_____

IV. Discuss your results and write your conclusions.

CONCLUSIONS

Experiment 3: Mass Matters

You need to design and perform an experiment to determine if mass is conserved during a chemical reaction. You can use any experimental approach you choose and the following experimental set up is only a suggestion.

Before you begin and to get you started, ask yourself the following questions:

(1) What chemical reactions am I aware of that produce products that can be collected and/or measured?

_____

_____

_____

(2) How would I collect the following types of products: a gas, a solid precipitate, a liquid?

_____

_____

_____

(3) How would I measure the following types of products if I could collect them: a gas, a solid precipitate, a liquid?

_____

_____

_____

Suggested Experiment: Splitting Water

As you know, the chemical formula for water is H_2O. This means that in a single molecule of water there are two hydrogen atoms for every oxygen atom. You can perform a decomposition reaction on water by passing an electric current through a cup full of baking soda water. The water molecules will split apart [decompose] into hydrogen gas and oxygen gas. The following set up will allow you to split water and measure the oxygen gas and hydrogen gas that is released. [*Challenge: Why do you need baking soda in the water?*]

WARNING

The suggested experiment generates hydrogen gas which is extremely flammable. Please use caution.

Experiment 3: _Splitting Water_   Date: _____

Objective: _To split water into hydrogen gas and oxygen gas using an electric current_

Hypothesis: _Because there are two hydrogen atoms for every oxygen atom, we should get twice as much hydrogen gas as oxygen gas._

Materials list:
two small test tubes
9 V battery
two strands of plastic coated wire [18 guage]
baking soda
water
cup, beaker, or jar
strong tape (such as duct tape)

Figure 1: Suggested Equipment

Experimental set up:

(1) Take the plastic coated wire and cut it into two pieces. With a wire stripper, strip about 4 cm off both ends of both pieces of wire. Make sure you have enough exposed wire to wrap around the battery leads.

(2) Next, fold one end of the wire and tuck it underneath the open end of the test tube. Repeat with the second wire and second test tube. Tape the wire to the outside of the test tube keeping the tucked end inside.

(3) In a separate container add some (1-2 Tbs.) baking soda to some (1-2 cups) warm water. Dissolve the baking soda completely.

(4) Pour the baking soda water into the beaker and fill each test tube with the baking soda water. Carefully invert the test tubes into the water-filled beaker without allowing too much air to rise up into the test tube.

(5) Tape the test tubes to the inside of the beaker along the top edge above the water. Now take the other ends of the wire and attach them to the battery. You should see bubbles beginning to form on the wires under the test tubes. These wires are "electrodes" and the water is split into hydgrogen gas on one electrode and oxygen gas on the other electrode. You are now collecting hydrogen gas in one test tube and oxygen gas in the other test tube.

(6) If you want to stop the reaction, disconnect one of the wires from one of the battery terminals.

(7) Try to see if you can determine which electrode is releasing hydrogen gas and which electrode is releasing oxygen gas.

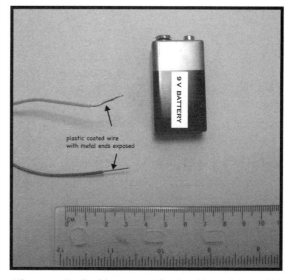

Figure 2: Battery and plastic wire with exposed ends.

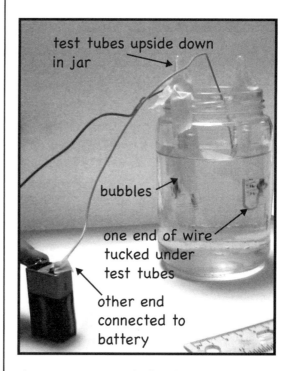

Figure 3: Suggested set up.

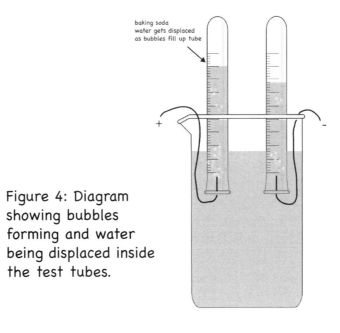

Figure 4: Diagram showing bubbles forming and water being displaced inside the test tubes.

Results

_____

_____

_____

_____

_____

_____

_____

_____

_____

_____

_____

_____

_____

_____

Conclusions

_____

_____

_____

_____

_____

_____

_____

_____

_____

_____

_____

_____

_____

_____

_____

_____

_____

_____

_____

_____

_____

_____

_____

Experiment 4: Acids and Bases

Design an experiment to determine the pH of several unknown liquids.

Hints: First, using red cabbage juice as an acid/base indicator, create your own pH scale. Using controls to determine what an acid "looks like" with the cabbage indicator and what a base "looks like" with the cabbage indicator.

Approximate pH and color change for red cabbage indicator:

approximate pH	2	4	6	8	10	12
color	red	purple	violet	blue	blue-green	green

Experiment: _____   Date: _____

Objective: _____

Materials List:

_____

_____

_____

_____

_____

Experimental setup:

_____

_____

_____

_____

Conclusions:

_____

_____

_____

_____

_____

_____

_____

_____

_____

_____

_____

_____

_____

Conclusions:

Experiment 5: Neutralization Reactions

Design an experiment to determine the endpoint of a neutralization reaction or
Perform a titration using a polyprotic acid.

Hints: Using the pH scale from Experiment 4 draw a color scale on the y-axis with the
corresponding pH for the titration. Use an acid and base that you measured the pH of in
Experiment 4. Remember that concentration matters. Do not use a very dilute solution with a
concentrated solution and visa versa.

Experiment: _____   Date: _____

Objective: _____

Hypothesis: _____

Materials List:

_____

_____

_____

_____

_____

Experimental setup:

_____

_____

_____

_____

_____

_____

Conclusions:

_____

_____

_____

_____

_____

_____

_____

_____

_____

_____

_____

_____

_____

Experiment 6: To Mix Or Not To Mix

Design an experiment to determine how well different household soaps form an emulsion.

Hints: Use both liquid soap and hard soap. Keep your measurements the same. To measure the emulsion use a clear narrow glass or test tube and a ruler. Vary your shaking times, but once you've decided on a time to shake [1 minute, 2 minutes etc.] keep it the same throughout the rest of your experiment.

Experiment:_____   Date_____

Objective:_____

Hypothesis:_____

Materials List:

_____

_____

_____

_____

_____

Experimental setup:

_____

_____

_____

_____

_____

_____

Conclusions:

Experiment 7: Pigments In Plants

Design an experiment to separate the pigments in leaves or flower petals.

Hints: Try different solvents such as rubbing alcohol, water, and a non-polar solvent such as GooGone.   Allow your solvents to interact with the leaves and flower petals for several hours or overnight, being careful not to let them evaporate.

Experiment:_____   Date _____

Objective: _____

Hypothesis: _____

Materials List:

_____

_____

_____

_____

Experimental setup:

_____

_____

_____

_____

_____

_____

Conclusions:

_____

_____

_____

_____

_____

_____

_____

_____

_____

_____

_____

_____

_____

_____

Experiment 8: Testing food for Carbohydrates and Lipids

Design an experiment to test different foods for the presence of carbohydrates and lipids.

You will need iodine and a brown paper sack.

Iodine reacts with carbohydrates turning them black. Iodine is very poisonous - DO NOT EAT
Lipids will make a brown paper sack translucent (clear).

Hints: First perform some "control" reactions.

Experiment:_____   Date_____

Objective: _____

Hypothesis:
_____

Materials List:

_____

_____

_____

_____

_____

Experimental setup:

_____

_____

_____

_____

_____

_____

Conclusions:

Experiment 9: Crosslinking Polymers

Design an experiment to test how polymer properties change as a function of crosslinking.

Hints: You know that Elmer's glue and Borax make a polymer. Determine what happens if you add different amounts of Borax to the Elmer's glue. Keeping the amount of glue consistent, vary the concentration of the Borax. Observe the polymer properties as a function of Borax concentration.

Experiment: _____   Date _____

Objective:

_____

Hypothesis:

_____

Materials List:

_____

_____

_____

_____

_____

Experimental setup:

_____

_____

_____

_____

_____

Conclusions:

Experiment 10: Which has more DNA? An onion or an egg?

In this experiment you will extract DNA from an onion and an egg and compare which has more DNA.

Hint: Follow the protocol for extracting DNA from food items. Try to be consistent with your measurements. Try not to lose too much of your experiment as you transfer your products from container to container.

Experiment: _____ Date _____

Objective: _____

Hypothesis: _____

Materials List:

_____

_____

_____

_____

_____

Experimental setup:

_____

_____

_____

_____

_____

_____

Conclusions:

REFERENCES

Lesson Summary: **DNA extraction**

This protocol describes a simple method for extracting DNA from living tissues.

Commentary:

This is a generalized protocol taken from a variety of references. It describes the general steps and rationale for nucleic acid extraction. The steps can be adapted to a particular sample by adjusting the volumes, and/or using a variety of different materials.

There are three overall steps for extracting nucleic acids from living tissues.

Step 1: Lysing the cells in the sample
Step 2: Separating the nucleic acids from the cell material
Step 3: Pulling out the nucleic acids.

Step 1: Lysing the cells in the sample

Recall that living tissues are made of cells and the nucleic acids are on the insides of cells. In order to extract nucleic acids from cells, the cells need to be opened, or *lysed*. The first step of the protocol opens, or lysis, the cells. This is accomplished by using a combination of detergents and enzymes (found in meat tenderizer, for use on animal cells.)

Step 2: Separating the DNA from the cell material

Once the cells are lysed, or broken open, there is a mixture of DNA, RNA, proteins, and other cell parts. The DNA and RNA needs to be separated from the proteins and other cell parts. This is accomplished in Step 2 by using alcohol. The nucleic acids are not soluable in the alcohol, so they precipitate out of the solution.

Step 3: Pulling out the DNA

After the DNA is separated from the cells parts, it can be extracted, or pulled out of the solution. This is accomplished in Step 3 using a wooden stick or Q-tip. Although all nucleic acids can be removed, only DNA survives the procedure. RNA is chewed up, or degraded, during the process by enzymes. DNA is more robust that RNA and is not easily degraded by enzymes.

MATERIALS

• *Suggested Samples*

The sample can be any living thing including but not limited to:

vegetable tissue, such as spinach, peas, green beans, broccoli, onions etc.

grains such as wheat germ, corn, oatmeal, seeds, or yeast

animal tissue such as eggs, chicken or beef livers, chicken hearts, etc.

• *Detergents (Liquid)*

Try any of the following:

• *Rubbing alcohol (isopropanol)*

• *Wooden stir stick or Q-tip*

• *Coffee filter*

• *Table salt*

STEP 1

LYSING THE SAMPLE

Part A: Prepare the sample for lysis

Put your sample in a blender and add twice as much cold water as sample [so for 1 cup of peas, add two cups of water], 1 teaspoon of table salt, and blend the sample on high speed until the sample is pureed [about 15 - 20 seconds].

Next pour your sample through a strainer or sieve into a glass jar or large test tube. This separates the larger plant or animal tissue from the cells. You should start with at least 1/4 cup of liquid.

Part B : Lysis

Add detergent to the cells to break them open. Use (1) tablespoon of detergent per cup of cell mixture. If you are lysing animal cells, add an additional teaspoon of meat tenderizer. Gently swirl the cell, water, detergent and meat tenderizer mixture being careful not to create foam. Allow the mixture to sit for 5 minutes gently swirling intermittently.

STEP 2

SEPARATING THE DNA FROM THE CELL MATERIAL

Next, tilting the jar or test tube, slowly add 1/4 cup of isopropanol per 1/4 cup of the cell-water mixture, pouring it down the inside of the jar or test tube. The alcohol will float to the top of the jar or test tube and the DNA will precipitate at the water-alcohol interface [the place where the alcohol and water meet]. This needs to be done slowly without agitating the mixture.

STEP 3

PULLING OUT THE DNA

Take the Q-tip or wooden stick and insert it into the alcohol layer. Gently touch the alcohol-water interface and swirl the stick or Q-tip pulling up slightly. The DNA will collect on the stick or Q-tip and there should be long strands visible. Continue spinning and collecting the DNA for a few seconds. Pull out the stick and place the DNA on a coffee filter to dry.

Troubleshooting is part of science. Almost no experiment works the first time. Many new discoveries are made by scientists when their experiments "fail."

TROUBLESHOOTING

FREQUENTLY ASKED QUESTIONS

What if I do not get at least 1/4 cup of liquid from Step 1, Part A, should I continue?

No. If you do not get at least 1/4 cup of material from Step 1 Part A blend the sample again adding more water. With smaller volumes, there may not be enough DNA extracted to visualize.

What if I do not see an alcohol-water inerface?

If you do not see an alcohol-water interface try adding more alcohol being careful not to agitate the sample. If you still do not see an interface, check the concentration of your alcohol and make sure it is not less than 70% alcohol. If your alcohol is more than 70% and you still do not see an interface, add twice the volume of alcohol to sample. You should eventually see an interface. If this fails, discard the sample and start over making sure you use water in Step 1.

What if I see foam?

Carefully remove the foam with an eyedropper without agitating the sample.

What if I do not get any DNA?

There could be several reasons you do not see any DNA.

1) You did not use enough starting material. Repeat the experiment and double the amount of starting material.
2) You did not use enough detergent. Repeat the experiment using more detergent.
3) You did not use the right kind of detergent. Repeat the experiment with a different detergent.
4) You did not let the sample sit long enough to break open the cells. Repeat the experiment and allow the sample to sit for a longer period of time.
5) You did not add detergent or enzyme to the sample. Repeat experiment adding enzyme or detergent or both.
6) You did not add enough alcohol. Add more alcohol.
7) The alcohol you added was not concentrated enough. Add 70-90% rubbing alcohol.
8) There is not enough salt in the water mixture to precipitate the sample. Add 1 teaspoon of table salt to your water-cell-alcohol mixture. Swirl. Add more rubbing alcohol until you see an interface and try to pull out the DNA.

DNA EXTRACTION

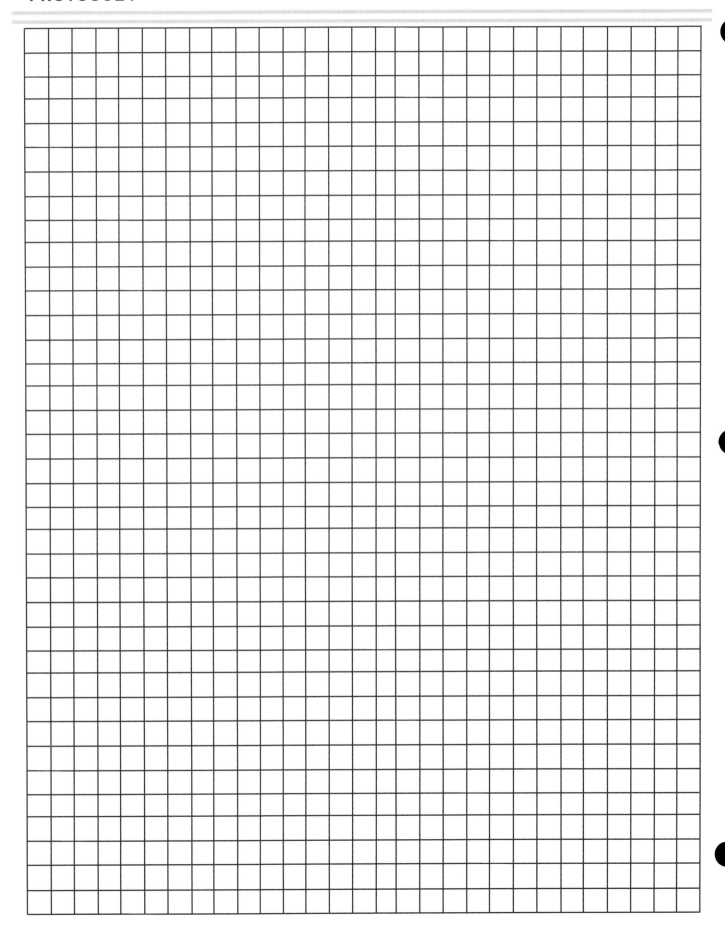

DNA EXTRACTION

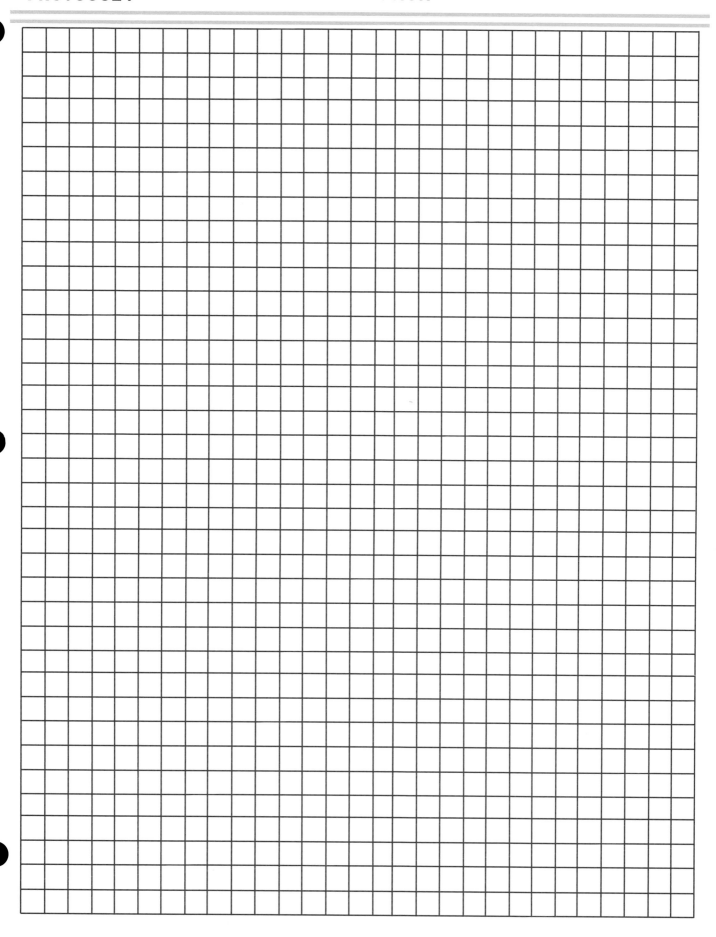

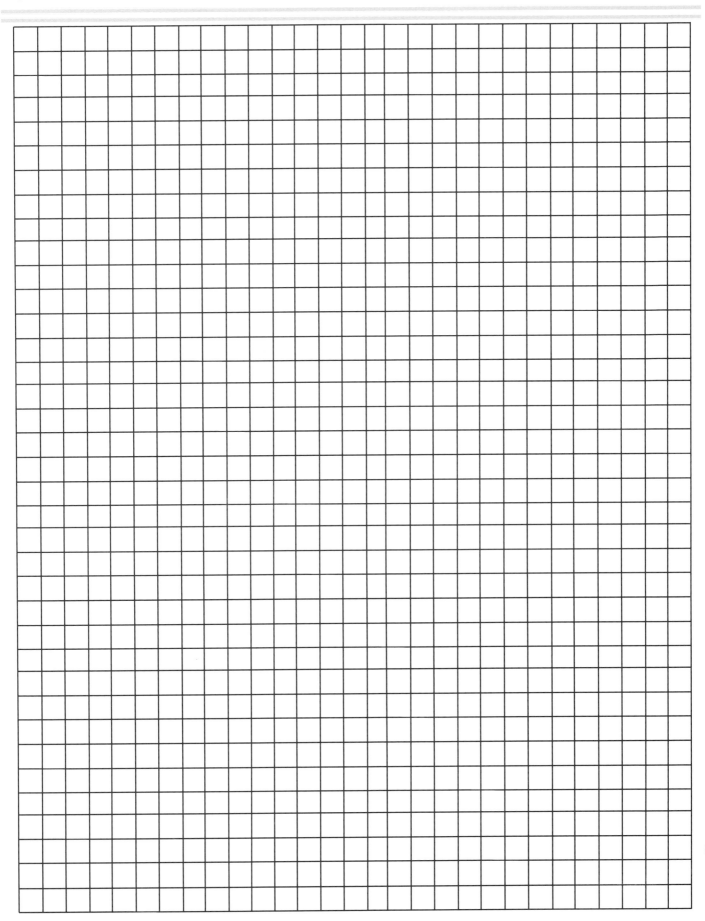

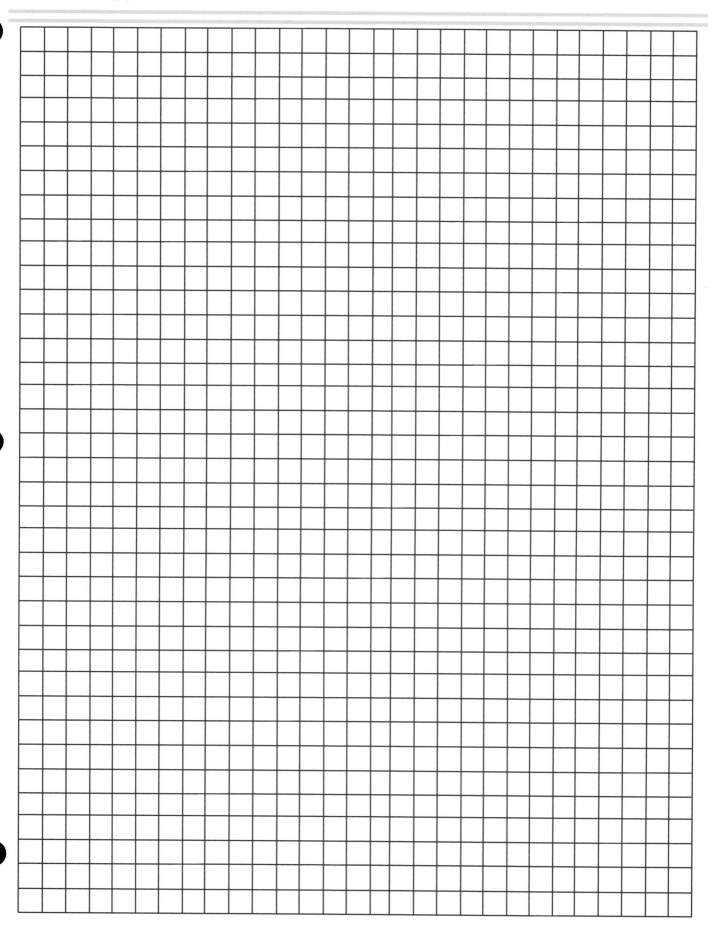

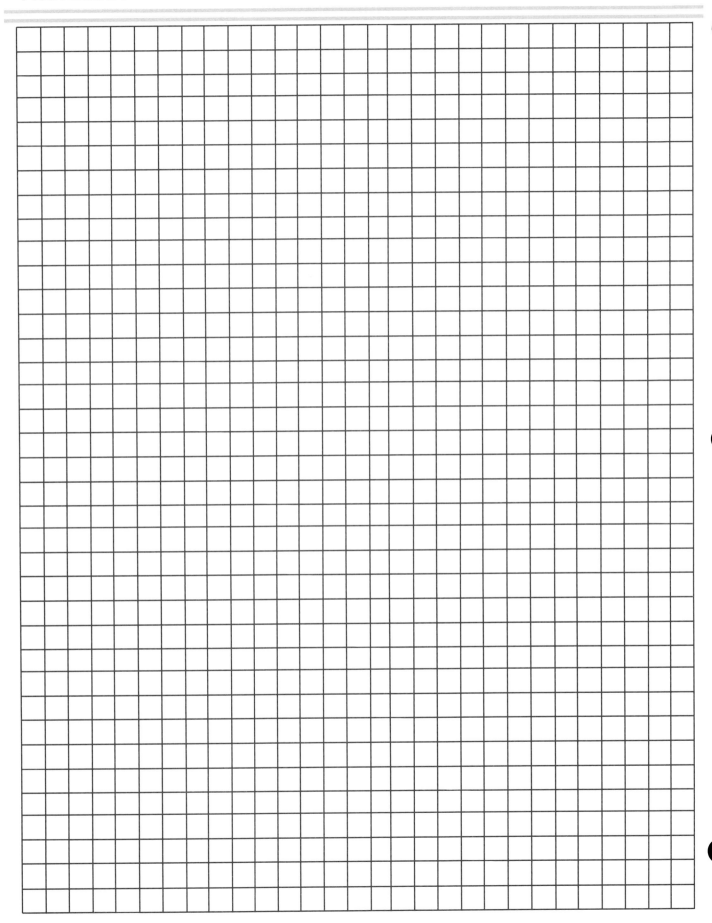

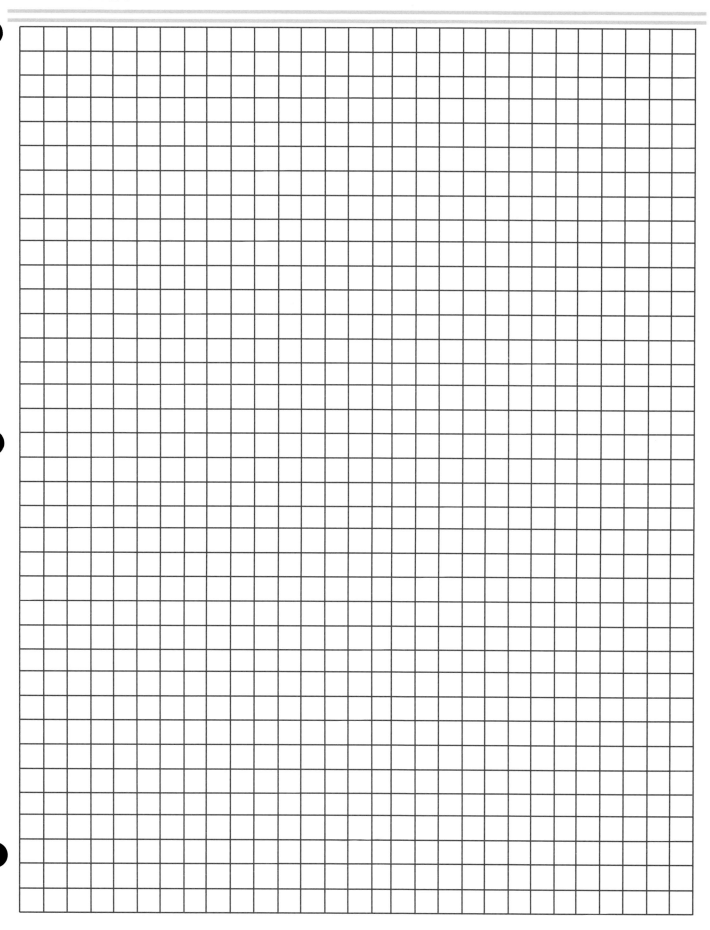

PROTOCOL I DNA EXTRACTION

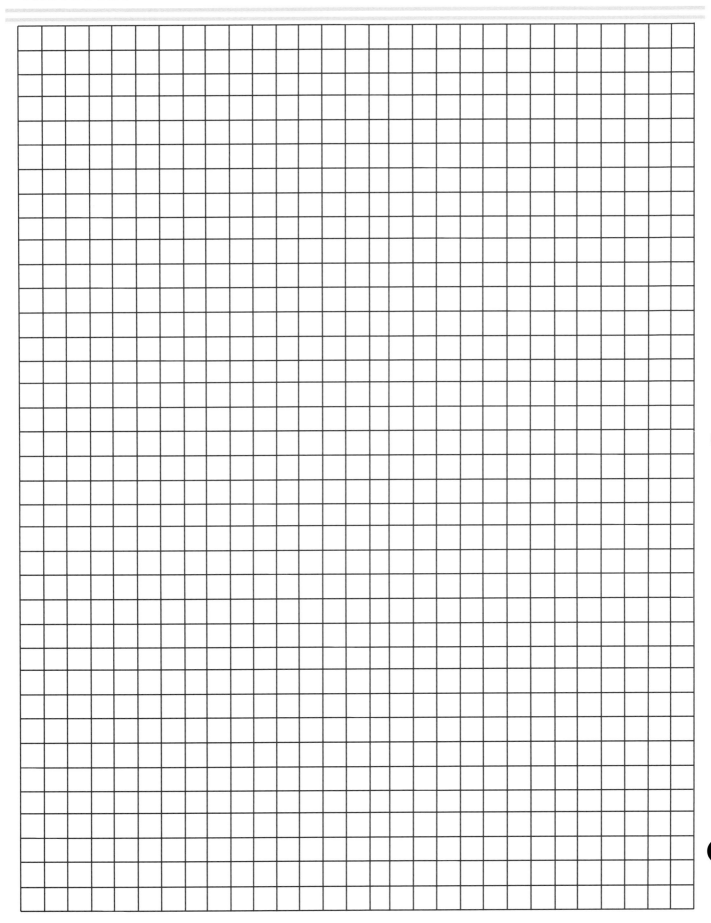

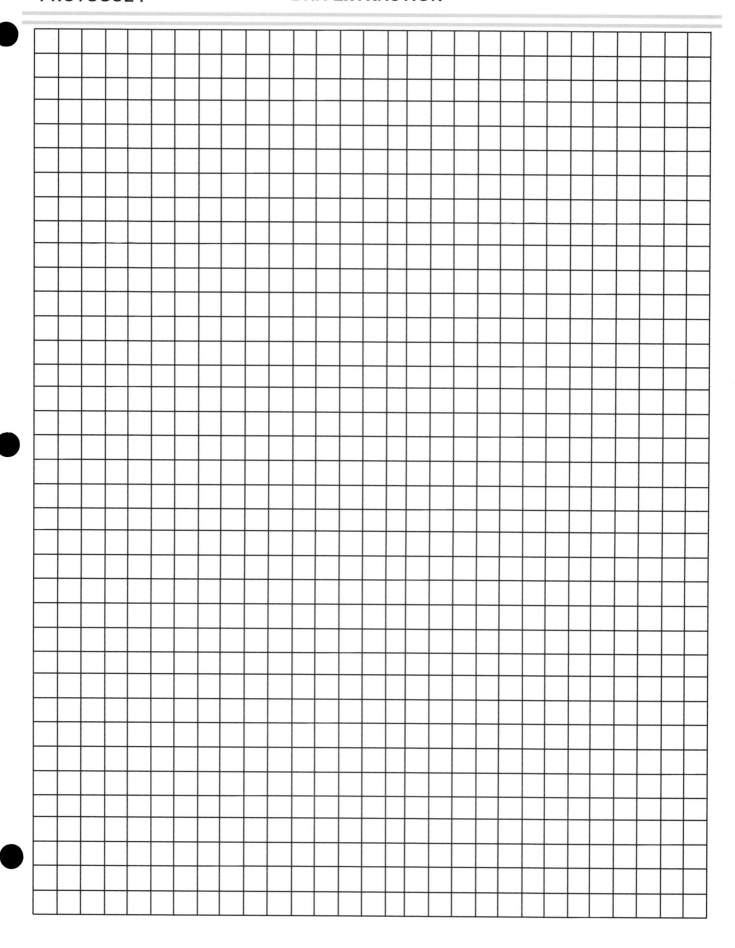

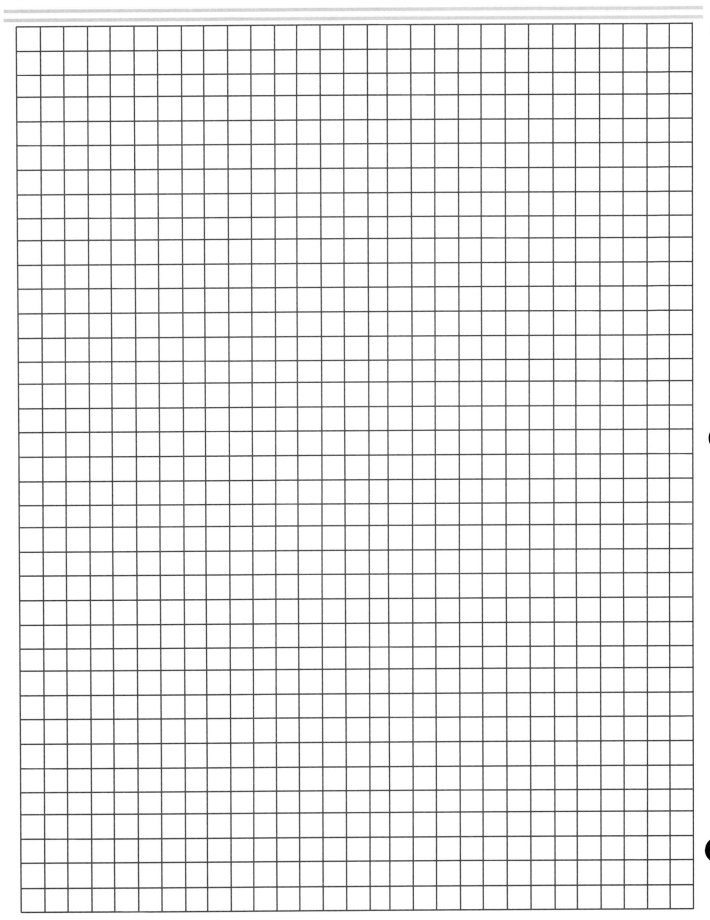

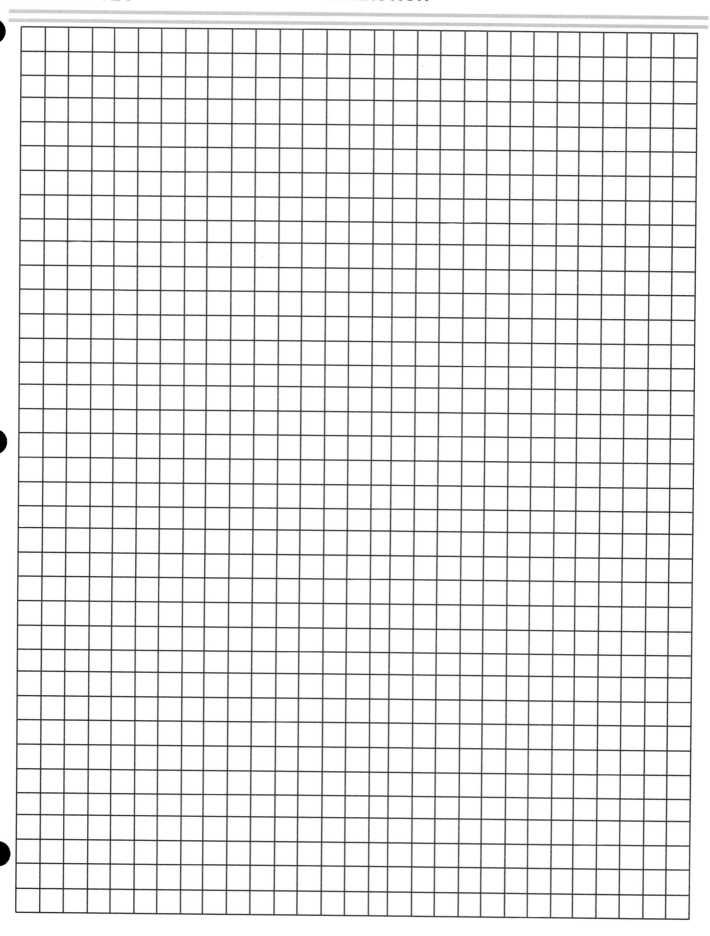

DNA EXTRACTION

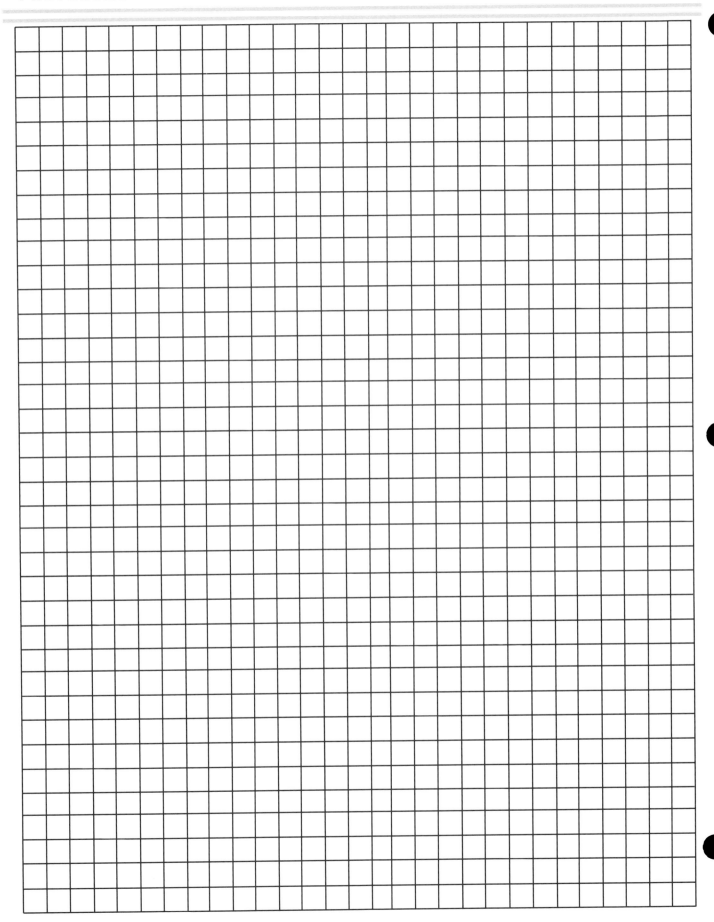

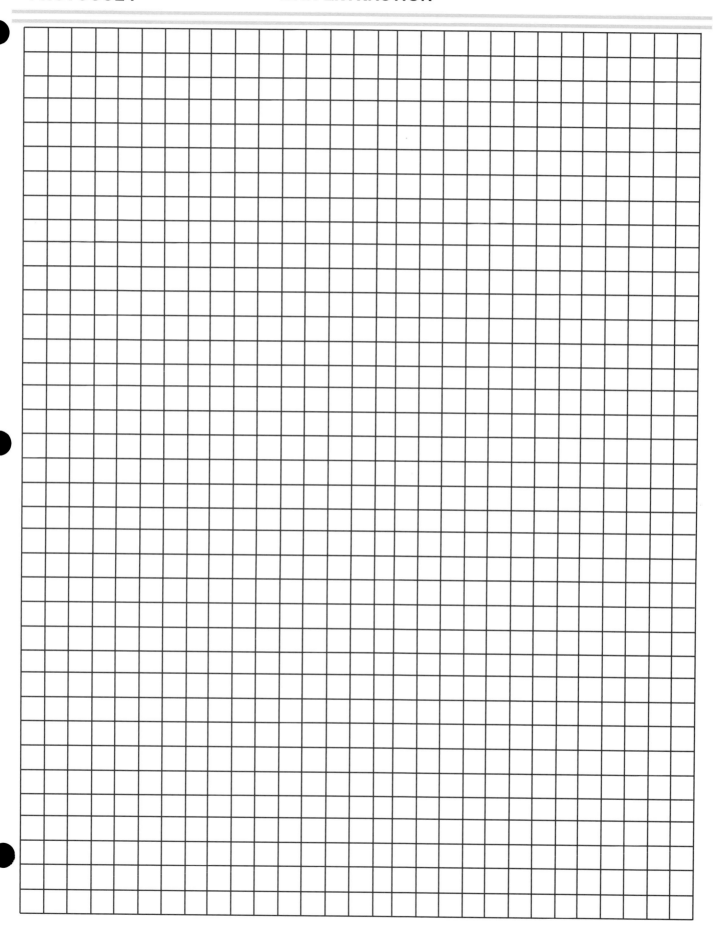

DNA EXTRACTION

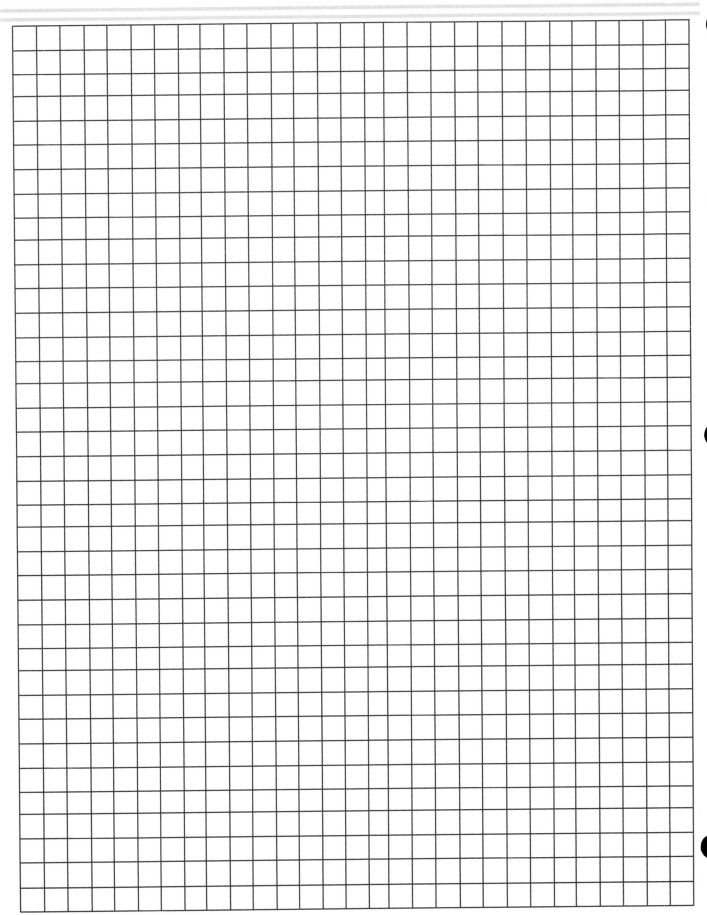

DNA EXTRACTION